OCR Poe
Confl
Anthology

The Ultimate Audio
Revision Guide

By
Emily Bird
and Jeff Thomas

How to answer a question when comparing an anthology poem to an unseen poem.

In the poetry section of your GCSE OCR Literature exam, you will be asked to:

a)   Compare a named poem from the OCR Anthology with an unseen poem.

AND

b)   Answer a related question on a different poem of your own choice from the OCR Anthology.

It is impossible to predict what poems will be set as the unseen component of your exam, so in this booklet, we have paired poems from within the Conflict cluster. This is designed to give you an insight into the comparison component of your question, as well as extending your knowledge of the poems themselves.

Plan your answer
Take a moment to jot down similarities/differences in the two poems.
Identify the surface story in the poems , see how they relate to each other, BUT don't fall into the trap of spending your time merely describing what happens in the poems.

Comparison is key
Ensure that you make constant comparisons throughout your work rather than discussing first one poem and then the other. Use comparative connectives such as 'whereas', 'likewise' and 'on the other hand' to draw your points together.

Compare the language
Look for language techniques such as metaphors, assonance or hyperbole and consider which poem is more effective at conveying its message through such techniques. Compare the narrators used in the poems, then state which narrator sounds more sympathetic/believable. Compare any autobiographical elements, state whether you think direct experience adds value to a poem? Consider the intended audience and purpose of both poems, and state which is more successful at communicating its purpose to its chosen audience.

Compare the titles
Which title is better in terms of conveying layers of meaning? Maybe one title is too literal, or too obscure to be truly effective, whilst the other perfectly sums up the poem.

Compare patterns in the form
Does one poem have a regular form and while the other is irregular? What effect does this have on the reader? Do both poems break patterns to create effects? If so, which poem does this more effectively?

Compare the structures
Do the poems employ similar use of stanzas, which poem is better at using its stanzas to build up its message? Do both poems use a volta? Were either of the turning points a surprise? If so, what effect does this have on the reader?   Does one poem use more enjambment or end stopped lines than the other? Which poem is more effective in its use of these techniques? Do both poems use repetition? If so, which poem does this more effectively? Compare the opening and closing images in the poems and discuss which you find more compelling.

Find your evidence
Ensure that you use quotations and refer directly to the poems to prove your points.

Compare how 'A Poison Tree' and 'Vergissmeinnicht' present the feeling of victory.

Introduction
- Both narrators have triumphed over an enemy, and while the protagonist of A Poison Tree is unashamedly '**glad**' of his victory, the main persona in Vergissmeinnicht feels a mixture of emotions, including something nearing contentment as well as a sense of sorrow.

Context
- Blake had a great interest in social reform and used poems like A Poison Tree to try and teach people good moral values, while Douglas wrote Vergissmeinnicht after his own experience of victory during the Battle of El Alamein.

Language
- The narrator in A Poison Tree is glad he's victorious because he hated his enemy. The <u>sibilance</u> in his language, '**sunned it with smiles**' helps to convey his hatred.
- The narrator in Vergissmeinnicht is relieved he's victorious because it was a case of life and death, he both feared and hated his enemy. The <u>sibilance</u> in his language, '**soldier sprawling in the sun**' communicates his negative emotions.

Form
- Blake's use of <u>rhyming couplets</u> gives his poem a 'sing-song' nursery rhyme sound, making it accessible in form, so that it could be used to teach children that taking delight in an unjustified victory is not good moral conduct.
- Douglas' use of <u>half-rhymes</u> and <u>para-rhymes</u> bring a sense of discomfort that reflects the narrator's feelings of disquiet as he both relishes his victory and at the same time, laments the horror of the situation.

Structure
- In Blake's poem, 14 out of 16 lines are <u>end-stopped</u>, giving it a measured quality, this allows the warning against gloating over a victory to be communicated with clarity.
- In Douglas' poem the narrator <u>juxtaposes</u> his callous reaction to the victory with the grief experienced by Steffi. This shows that the narrator knows his reactions are distorted, and by the <u>final stanza</u>, his attitude has become more reflective.

How do the poems 'Envy' and 'Boat Stealing' explore the theme of self-knowledge?

Introduction
- The narrator in *Envy* preaches that a better understanding of oneself will bring contentment, while the narrator in *Boat Stealing* finds that gaining self-knowledge can be a frightening experience.

Context
- Both poets were part of the Romantic literary movement and both feature the key Romantic theme of nature as they explore the issue of self-knowledge.

Language
- Lamb uses the <u>extended metaphor</u> of the rose tree to argue that with **'care and culture all may find'** their good points and come to a better understanding of themselves.
- Wordsworth uses the <u>extended metaphor</u> of the geographical features around the lake to show that as someone explores their limits, they may find that the new experiences can be daunting and **'trouble'** their **'dreams'**.

Form
- Lamb's poem takes the form of a <u>lesson</u>, it sounds confident in its message that self-knowledge brings contentment.
- Wordsworth's <u>epic</u>, from which *Boat Stealing* is taken, reflects the fact that the poet acknowledges our inner selves are complex places and take time to understand.

Structure
- *Envy* <u>finishes</u> by saying that the talents found within will be **'rare'**, this leaves the reader feeling that if they do seek self-knowledge they will be rewarded with the realisation that they are unique and special.

- *Boat Stealing* <u>ends on a more sombre note</u> than *Envy*. The narrator says that his new understanding has left his thoughts in **'darkness'**. This suggests that the more someone reflects upon themselves and their place in the world, the more they come to understand that they are flawed, while the world itself is a complicated place.

How is the theme of turmoil key to the poems 'Boat Stealing' and 'Honour Killing'?

Introduction

- Up to the point in the poem, the narrator of *Boat Stealing* has had a sheltered life without turmoil, but now realises that the world is a complex place, and at times his life will be tumultuous, while the narrator in *Honour Killing* has endured a lifetime of turmoil, living under an oppressive regime, but prepares to leave this behind and escape.

Context

- Wordsworth, like other Romantic writers, looked to explore individual experiences and emotions, while Dharker's poetry aims to expose the injustices in the modern world.

Language

- Wordsworth uses the oxymoron, '**troubled pleasure**' to shows that stealing the boat fills the narrator with conflicting emotions and suggests that he is half expecting to encounter turmoil during his adventure.
- Dharker uses the '**black coat**' to symbolise the turmoil of the narrator's past, the fact that she was '**born wearing it**' tells the reader she has suffered all her life.

Form

- Both poets work with unrhymed verse in order to produce an unostentatious form that won't overshadow the narrators' exploration of the turmoil in their lives.

Structure

- On line 6 of *Boat Stealing*, the narrator '**struck**' and '**struck again**' as he begins to row out into the lake, showing the excitement he feels as he steals the boat. Later, this language is repeated but this time the action shows that he now feels turmoil, not excitement, as a result of seeing the dark peak. The repetition contrasts the narrator's state of mind before and after his epiphany.
- In *Honour Killing*, the words '**Let's see**' are repeated and are used to emphasize that the narrator is intrigued and excited by the prospect of her new life, free from turmoil.

How are the enemies portrayed in 'The Destruction of Sennacherib' and 'A Poison Tree'?

Introduction

- In *The Destruction of Sennacherib* the enemy force is portrayed as an organised and merciless army, and yet, it proves to be no match against the '**Angel of Death**'.
- In *A Poison Tree*, the enemy is portrayed as so fascinating the narrator can't stop thinking about him '**day and night**'.

Context

- Byron references a specific enemy by alluding to the Biblical accounts of Sennacherib's attack on Jerusalem.
- The enemy in Blake's poem is referred to as the '**foe**' making him anonymous and therefore allows Blake to use the narrative as a cautionary tale applicable to everyone.

Language

- Byron uses the <u>simile</u> '**like a wolf**' to describe the Assyrians, making them sound fierce; it also dehumanises them and brings them down to the level of beasts.
- Blake <u>implies</u> that the enemy in his poem is both sly and covetous. He '**stole**' into the garden under cover of darkness when '**the night had veil'd the pole**', showing that his actions are planned out as well as nefarious.

Form

- Both poems employ <u>rhyming couplets</u> throughout giving the verses a very regular form.

Structure

- In Byron's poem, the <u>volta</u> appears half way through stanza two, before this, the Assyrian enemy seems powerful and proud, '**gleaming in purple and gold**', but afterwards they are shown to be no match against the power of God and lay '**distorted and pale**' in the wake of the Angel's attack.
- In Blake's poem, a <u>volta</u> is introduced after the first two lines, when the focus switches from anger between friends, to anger between enemies. The fact that this takes up the majority of the poem reflects the fact that the narrator is consumed by thoughts of his enemy.

What do the poems 'There's a Certain Slant of Light' and 'Punishment' reveal about human nature?

Introduction
- Dickinson's poem explores the idea that it is human nature to feel overwhelmed by our existence, while *Punishment* shows that human nature can be both cruel and creative.

Context
- Although Dickinson was a prolific poet, she did not desire her work to be published; this desire for privacy is reflected in her poem, with its theme of isolation.
- Heaney's poem looked to explore the underlying human nature that fuelled The Troubles of Northern Ireland.

Language
- Dickinson finds darkness in symbolism that is more traditionally used to represent positive feelings; she turns a **'slant of light'** into a metaphor for oppression. Revealing there is a tendency in humans to look on the dark side.
- In Heaney's poem **'oak-bone'** and **'brain-firkin'** are examples of kennings, a common feature of Old English poetry. These remind the reader that although people were brutal, it was also in their nature to be creative.

Form
- Dickinson's poem is hymn-like and enhances the idea that it is human nature to try and develop a sense of spirituality.
- The even four line stanzas in Heaney's poem give it a measured form and reflects the moderated way the narrator tries to work through observations about humans.

Structure
- The structure of Dickinson's poem is broken through her use of dashes, which arrest the flow of language and suggest that much is left unsaid as the narrator struggles to order her thoughts and feelings about herself and human nature.
- In Heaney's poem **'like a stubble of black corn'** is used to show that the girl's hair was shaved as part of the humiliating ritual that took place before her execution. This episode foreshadows the modern day Irish women who are **'cauled in tar'**. Such structuring draws the past and present together in order to show that mankind has not developed.

Do either 'The Man He Killed' or 'Phrase Book' present a sense of hope for mankind?

Introduction
- Both poems present an ambiguous message regarding hope. They show that gentle people can be killers and that although thoughts of love can arise during wartime, they can also be ground '**into dust/ into dust.**'

Context
- Hardy was a prolific writer of novels and poetry and is known for creating literature that has a bleak outlook on life.
- *Phrase Book* highlights the fact that mankind is always developing its technology, but it squanders this on making weapons and reporting on wars in a lurid manner, suggesting that there is little hope.

Language
- In Hardy's poem, line 9 ends with a dash in order to create a pause in the poem that reflects the <u>pause in the veteran's speech</u>. This signals that the man needs to think about why he shot the other man dead, and this senseless killing creates a feeling of hopelessness.
- In *Phrase Book*, <u>military terms</u> such as '**Stealthed**' and '**Cleaned**' are <u>euphemisms</u> for casualties and show that language is used to disguise the truth so that people can continue waging war, this facility to deceive brings a sense of hopelessness to the poem.

Form
- Both poems are <u>monologues</u> and the reader must remember that they present just one point of view.

Structure
- In Hardy's poem, the <u>enjambment</u> from line 12 to 13 links stanzas 3 and 4. This shows that as the man reflects on his past he can no longer contain his feelings, the overflowing lines symbolize his overflowing thoughts as he struggles with the sense of hopelessness that killing a fellow human has brought.
  - The <u>final stanza</u> of *Phrase Book* contains a <u>rapid succession</u> of questions, they are used to intensify the feeling of disorientation, reflecting the idea that war, and the coverage of war, brings only more questions, certainly no answers.

What do 'Anthem For Doomed Youth' and 'There's a Certain Slant of Light' have to say about religion?

Introduction

- Both poems imply that at times, religion fails to provide comfort or solace for the faithful.

Context

- The horrors of The Great War caused may people to doubt their religion.
- Dickinson was brought up a Calvinist, but in adult life decided to stop attending public worship, whilst still retaining a sense of faith. This struggle with defining spirituality is evident in the poem as religion is a key theme.

Language

- Owen presents the trenches as a godless place where church bells are replaced by the racket of gunfire and then scathingly suggests that the rituals of religion are '**mockeries**' anyway; it doesn't matter that the men have no last rites as their deaths are senseless, no matter what's done to commemorate their passing. He implies that there was no sanctity of life in the trenches.
- In Dickinson's poem, stanza two begins with the oxymoron '**Heavenly Hurt**', this language suggests that even though religion brings suffering, it is worth trying to find '**Meanings**', within the framework of a faith.

Form

- Owen's poem is an elegy and its personal observations commemorate the fallen soldiers in a way that religion, as an institution, cannot.
- In terms of its metre and rhyme scheme, Dickinson's poem reflects the form found in many hymns. This form enhances the religious undercurrent found in the poem.

Structure

- In *Anthem For Doomed Youth*, both the octet and the sestet begin with a question that, in part, is used to challenge the role of religion.
- Dickinson's poem opens with the imagery of the oppressive light as it streams from heaven in order to establish religion as a key theme.

Explore how 'Vergissmeinnicht' and 'The Man He Killed' depict the effects of being a soldier.

Introduction

- Both poems depict soldiers as they reflect on what it feels like to have been the victor in a kill-or-be-killed situation.

Context

- Despite being a dutiful soldier, Douglas privately thought that combat was destroying his humanity and this is evident in the cold, callous tone of the narrator in *Vergissmeinnicht*.
- Hardy had a particular interest in the Napoleonic Wars and interviewed veterans of this conflict. It is reasonable to think that these conversations informed him of the perspectives of the common soldier.

Language

- Douglas uses the simile '**like the entry of a demon**' to show that soldiers have to face hellish situations, and these can harden them, so that in the case of the soldier in the poem he is able to survey his dead enemy '**almost with content**'.
- In Hardy's poem, the soldier exclaims how '**quaint and curious war is!**' This use of litotes suggests that the man is so overwhelmed by his experience of war that he struggles to find the right words to describe it. His understatement shows that words fail to describe the horrors he's seen and done.

Form

- In *Vergissmeinnicht* the rhyme scheme falls into a pattern, only to break this and take up a different arrangement, arguably reflecting the chaotic situations that soldiers face.
- Hardy's poem has a sophisticated form. It never deviates from rhyming alternate lines. Lines 1, 2 and 4 of each quatrain uses an iambic trimeter rhythm, while line 3 of each quatrain uses an iambic tetrameter. This refined form elevates the seemingly straightforward language that the man uses to express himself, so that the work becomes profound and enduring, not just an anecdote of one soldier.

Structure

- Both poems begin with a sense of mystery, then events are revealed piece by piece as both soldiers try to explain what it is like to kill someone. This gradual reveal brings tension to the structure.

How does remembrance feature in 'What Were They Like' and 'Anthem For Doomed Youth'?

Introduction

- Both poets show that the act of remembrance has the most significance when it is performed by people emotionally close to the fallen.

Context

- Levertov was part of the anti-war movement in the U.S. and campaigned for the withdrawal of U.S. troops from Vietnam.
- Remembrance Day takes place on the 11th November in order to commemorate those who have fallen in conflict.

Language

- In Levertov's poem, the second speaker uses <u>adverbs</u> like '**perhaps**' to show they're not sure about their answers. This emphasizes the idea that the war against the Vietnamese was so ferocious, they have almost been wiped out and it is hard to remember what they were like as so little was left.
- Having railed against the inadequacy of religion in the <u>octet</u>, Owen finds that there is sincerity in the '**pallor of girls' brows**', so while the institution of the church provides nothing, the true emotions of friends and relatives ensures that every fallen soldier is commemorated.

Form

- Levertov's poem is formed of questions and answers. This is used to show that if a race of people is wiped out, it becomes hard to remember what they were like, until ultimately remembrance is replace with a history lesson.
- *Anthem For Doomed Youth* is a <u>requiem</u> designed to ensure that everyone remembers the horrors of World War I.

Structure

- In Levertov's poem, '**It is not remembered**' is <u>repeated twice</u> in the second stanza to emphasize the fact that the war has destroyed the entire Vietnamese nation; there is nobody left to remember details about them.
- In Owen's poem, the <u>octet and the sestet both begin with a question</u>, which Owen then goes on to answer. This structure makes the reader think, while at the same time allowing Owen to convey his opinions and memories.

Compare the theme of destruction in 'Lament' and 'The Destruction of Sennacherib'.

Introduction
- Clarke's poem laments the destruction of the natural world while Byron's poem celebrates the destruction of an invading army.

Context
- During the First Gulf War, retreating Iraqi troops opened up oil valves as a method of slowing down the U.S. forces that were pursuing them. This caused the biggest oil spill in history and devastated natural habitats in the Persian Gulf.
- The Temple of Baal, which is mentioned in the last stanza of Byron's poem was partially destroyed by ISIS in 2015, showing that war and conflict is an ever present problem.

Language
- In *Lament*, the <u>metaphor</u> of the '**mortal stain**' conveys that the destruction is deadly, and impossible to wash away.
- In Byron's poem, the <u>simile</u> '**melted like snow**' is used to emphasize the fact that for all their '**might**', the Assyrians were no match the Angel of Death. This idea is intensified with the final phrase '**the glance of the Lord!**' Proving that God needed to make barely any effort in order to destroy Sennacherib's army.

Form
- *Lament* takes the form of an <u>elegy</u>, and lists all the destruction in the natural world caused by the First Gulf War.
- The <u>metre</u> in Byron's poem produces a very <u>buoyant rhythm</u>, and could reflect the jubilant feelings of those who have escaped being destroyed by Sennacherib.

Structure
- In line 18 of *Lament*, the sun is '**veiled**' but <u>by next line</u> it has

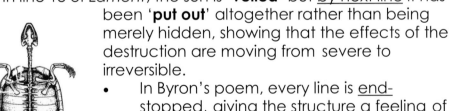

  been '**put out**' altogether rather than being merely hidden, showing that the effects of the destruction are moving from severe to irreversible.
    - In Byron's poem, every line is <u>end-stopped</u>, giving the structure a feeling of containment, reflecting the idea that the Assyrian soldiers could not escape from the destructive powers of the Angel of Death.

How do 'Punishment' and 'What Were They Like' convey a theme of injustice?

Introduction

- *Punishment* shows injustice has always been a feature of society, while *What Were They Like?* shows that entire nations can be as vulnerable to injustice as individuals.

Context

- *Punishment* links the bog body to Irish women who had relationships with British soldiers, showing society is still unjust.
- America was involved in Vietnam's affairs from 1955 to 1973. Many Americans saw this involvement as unjust.

Language

- The '**Little adulteress**' in Heaney's poem <u>refers</u> to the woman accused of adultery in John, Chapter 8. Jesus pronounces that anyone without sin is free to stone her to death; her accusers realised that this rules them out so they slip away.
- This <u>allusion</u> is picked up later when the narrator says he would have cast '**stones of silence**', he knew women were suffering injustice but kept quiet. He didn't judge/defend as he had his own sins and didn't want these revealed.
- The <u>imagery of nature</u> is used throughout Levertov's poem to characterize the Vietnamese as a gentle nation. The Vietnamese spent their time surrounded by '**rice and bamboo**' under skies of '**peaceful clouds**'. Such imagery suggests that the Vietnamese were innocent and suffered great injustices at the hands of their attackers.

Form

- The <u>even four line stanzas</u> in Heaney's poem provide a <u>measured feeling to the form</u> allowing the narrator to carefully work through feelings about injustice.
- The <u>question and answer form</u> of Levertov's poem makes the reader think about the consequences of the injustices suffered by the Vietnamese.

Structure

- *Punishment* <u>begins</u> with the narrator empathising with the girl from the bog, he can '**feel**' what it was like for her to suffer the injustices she went through.
- In Levertov's poem, the line '**Sir, their light hearts turned to stone**' is <u>end-stopped</u> in order to give the reader a pause, so that they have time to reflect on the effects of the injustice.

What do the poems 'Flag' and 'Partition' have to say about national identity?

Introduction
- *Flag* warns individuals not to lose their own identity within that of a national identity, while *Partition* shows that individuals can love their nation and still retain their identity.

Context
- Much of Agard's poetry is concerned with national identity and the cultural effects of patriotism.
- The title of *Partition* refers to the 1947 partitioning of British Colonial India into the independent countries of Pakistan and India.

Language
- In *Flag*, the <u>image</u> '**flying across a field**' is used to show that nationalism is tied up with land ownership and power.
- The <u>rhetorical question</u> the mother asks at the end of the poem shows that she has a deep love for her nation and laments the fact that it was damaged during partitioning.

Form
- Agard uses a <u>sophisticated rhyme scheme</u>. In the first stanza, lines 1 and 3 have a <u>full rhyme</u> with '**breeze/knees**'. In the second stanza, lines 1 and 3 are linked through the <u>assonance</u> of '**pole/bold**'. In stanza three, '**tent/relent**' sees a return to <u>full rhyme</u>. And in stanza four, lines 1 and 3 have a <u>jarring half-rhyme</u> with '**field/bleed**'. This alternation between full rhyme and alternatives reflects the content of the poem, some people fully buy into the symbolism of their flag and the identity it represents, while others see the symbolism as disingenuous.
- *Partition* is written in <u>free verse</u> in order to allow the narrators to recall their memories in a natural sounding way.

Structure
- In *Flag*, <u>every stanza begins with a question</u>, which is then answered, and this structure encourages readers to question the concept of national identity.
- In *Partition*, from line 27 until the end, the <u>fractured nature of the structure</u> seems to express that the mother is sobbing as she thinks about what happened to her nation.

What do the poems 'Phrase Book' and 'Flag' have to say about International Relations?

Introduction

- *Phrase Book* shows that conflict happens when countries don't understand each other, while *Flag* suggests that once borders are drawn and flags are raised, conflict is inevitable.

Context

- *Phrase Book* was written in response to the First Gulf War, where a coalition of troops, including Britain and America, forced the invading Iraqi army out of Kuwait.
- Agard was resident in his home country of Guiana when it gained independence in 1966, showing he has first hand experience of how international relations affect lives.

Language

- A *Phrase Book* only allows someone to 'get by' in a foreign country but its use doesn't amount to being able to speak the language or understand the culture. This is an extended metaphor for trying to communicate with other nations.
- In *Flag*, the alliteration in '**nation to its knees**' emphasizes that large groups of people will be utterly loyal to their flag, sometimes to the exclusion of the interests of other nations.

Form

- Shapcott's poem often slips into its phrasebook form, and this 'language barrier effect' serves as a metaphor for the difficulty in communicating with other nations.
- Agard deviates from an established rhyme scheme in the final stanza. Here, the first line is left unrhymed, while the final two lines are rounded off with a rhyming couplet, in order to emphasize that the dialogue has reached a definite conclusion even though talks have failed.

Structure

- Key elements of *Phrase Book* are structured around the questions that the narrator asks and makes the reader question their own understanding of how international relations work or fail to work.
- In the first four stanzas of *Flag* '**It's just a piece of cloth**' is an angry refrain used to emphasize the fact that people sometimes put so much importance on their own nation that they fail to consider the needs of others.

Are the narrators of 'Honour Killing' and 'Envy' good role models in the way they avoid conflict?

Introduction

- The narrator of *Honour Killing* sets the example of taking positive action instead of causing conflict, while the narrator of *Envy* advocates that everyone should search inside themselves to become the best person they can be.

Context

- Dharker wrote *Honour Killing* in response to a particular case where a woman was shot by a family member and the Pakistan senate refused to act against the murderers.
- Although *Envy* was written for children, its message is applicable to people of all ages. In the modern world, surrounded by polished social media profiles, it can be easy to lose sight of true inner qualities.

Language

- In Dharker's poem, the narrator <u>subverts</u> the concept of an honour killing, so that instead of trying to get revenge, she is slaying the customs and laws of her past to obtain freedom.
- Lamb presents a very <u>hopeful tone</u>, saying that '**all may find**' their inner worth if only they take a little time to look.

Form

- In *Honour Killing*, the protagonist's act of stripping down is for herself and nobody else, therefore, this is a <u>soliloquy</u>, a private experience that she narrates to herself with a stately sense of wonder.
- *Envy* has a <u>consistent rhyme scheme</u>, giving it a steady tone that compliments the wholesome message that it imparts.

Structure

- In *Honour Killing*, the narrator uses the pause at the end of line 31 to suggest that her '**plotting**' may be for revenge, but then the <u>enjambment</u> quickly pulls the reader onto the final line to reveal that she is actually '**plotting**' in a

  cartographical sense as she plans where to travel to in her '**new geography**', proving that she is a good role model.
- *Envy* is structured around a logical argument that <u>builds up step by step</u>, using the extended metaphor of the rose-tree. This allows Lamb to set out her sound advice in a clear way.

Consider the theme of regret in 'Partition' and 'Lament'.

Introduction

- In *Partition* the mother bitterly regrets that she did not help others during the partitioning of India crisis, while in *Lament* the narrator regrets all the harm done to the natural world due to events that happened during the First Gulf War.

Context

- Cyril Radcliffe, a British lawyer, was given the task of drawing up the boundaries for India and Pakistan even though he had little knowledge of the area. He is the '**man**' that the mother refers to on line 34 in *Partition*.
- Clarke states that she used media images connected to the First Gulf War as source material for *Lament*. These images included cormorants covered in oil.

Language

- In *Partition*, the daughter repeats that her mother '**stood**' in her garden and this <u>verb</u> proves that she was inactive during the crisis, paralysed by her fear, something which she now regrets.
- Clarke uses the <u>metaphor</u> of '**funeral silk**' to show that the black oil that clogs the cormorant's feathers will kill it, and that each death is beyond regrettable.

Form

- *Partition* is formed of <u>recalled memories</u> and a <u>monologue</u> to give a personal perspective on the partitioning of India, where the speaker demonstrates feelings of regret.
- *Lament* is a <u>requiem</u> for all the life that was harmed in the First Gulf War.

Structure

- In *Partition*, on line 16 the mother '**wished**' she could make herself go and help those in need and this emotion is <u>repeated</u> again on line 27. This highlights the overarching feeling of the poem, which is that of regret.
- In *Lament*, every stanza begins with the words '**For the...**' and each time, this <u>refrain</u> brings the reader back to the title *Lament*, this reinforces the emotions of regret, sorrow and grief connected with the events of the First Gulf War.

Suggested poems to use when preparing for the question where you compare unseen poetry and anthology poetry.

The following is a list of suggested poems that would be suitable for a GCSE pupil to use when revising for the anthology/unseen poetry comparison question.

Try pairing these with poems from your OCR Conflict Anthology cluster and finding similarities and differences.

Arms and the Boy	Wilfred Owen
Bayonet Charge	Ted Hughes
Belfast Confetti	Ciaran Carson
Catrin	Gillian Clarke
Checking Out Me History	John Agard
Cousin Kate	Christina Rossetti
Dulce et Decorum Est	Wilfred Owen
Exposure	Wilfred Owen
Half Caste	John Agard
Kamikaze	Beatrice Garland
London	William Blake
My Last Duchess	Robert Browning
No Problem	Benjamin Zephaniah
Ozymandias	Percy Bysshe Shelley
Poppies	Jane Weir
Remains	Simon Armitage
Storm on the Island	Seamus Heaney
The Charge of the Light Brigade	Alfred Tennyson
The Class Game	Mary Casey
The Emigree	Carole Rumens
Tissue	Imtiaz Dharker
War Photographer	Carol Ann Duffy
War Photographer	Carole Satyamurti

N.B. These poems are not on the OCR syllabus.

Glossary of Key Terms

Alliteration	Repetition of consonant sounds.
Allusion	A reference to a literary, historical, classical or mythic person, place or event.
Ambiguity	When two or more meanings are present.
Archaic	Language that is no longer in modern usage.
Assonance	Repetition of vowel sounds.
Colloquial	Informal language used in everyday speech.
Couplet	A pair of rhymed lines.
Caesura	A pause, usually signalled by punctuation.
Conceit	A form of metaphor that fuses surprising elements.
Double entendre	Language that has a double meaning, where one meaning is innocent, while the other is risqué.
End-stopped	When the phrase/sentence ends at the end of a line.
Enjambment	When a phrase or sentence runs over the end of one line and into the next.
Extended metaphor	When a metaphor is reused and elaborated upon.
Euphemism	Innocent sounding language with an underlying meaning that refers to something vulgar.
Homonym	Same spelling but different meanings.
Hyperbole	Over exaggeration for poetic effect.
In medias res	When the action is already taking place at the start of a poem.
Juxtaposed	When two ideas are placed side by side for effect.
Litotes	Extreme understatement.
Metaphor	When a comparison is made without an explicit connection being pointed out.
Motif	A reoccurring image.
Octave	The first 8 lines in a sonnet.
Onomatopoeia	When the sound of the spoken language resembles the meaning of the language.
Oxymoron	When two opposing ideas are placed next to each other.
Pathos	Language that creates feelings of pity and sorrow.
Personification	Giving human qualities to non-human features.
Polysemantic	Having many meanings.
Pun	Wordplay where a homonym is used to give two meanings.
Quatrain	A group of four lines, usually with a rhyme scheme.
Refrain	When a line or phrase is repeated at set intervals.
Rhetorical question	A question that is used to make the reader think rather than respond with an answer.
Rhyme scheme	A set pattern of rhymed lines.
Sestet	The last six lines in a sonnet.
Simile	A comparison that uses the words 'as' or 'like'.
Stanza	A unit of sense within a poem.
Synecdoche	When a part is used to represent the whole.
Volta	Turning point.

About us...

Jeff Thomas

Until recently, Jeff worked as a history teacher, specialising in alternative teaching methods. Jeff has also worked alongside the University of Sussex in the role of PGCE mentor, and has trained numerous student teachers. With the ever growing success of Revision Rocks, Jeff has now stopped teaching, in order to work full-time on developing new and exciting revision aids. Jeff also works as an expert examiner for Edexcel.

Jeff has appeared on: BBC 5 live, BBC Sussex, Kent, London and Surrey to talk about cutting edge revision techniques and Revision Rocks. Jeff has also been featured in the Times Educational Supplement (TES) on two occasions, in relation to revising through song. Jeff has also made many radio appearances for the BBC to discuss issues relating to history and secondary education, which he says makes him feel very important within the world of teaching.

Emily Bird

Emily trained as an English teacher, but has also taught other subjects including: History, Psychology and R.E. Emily developed her teaching career in the area of SEN, and has a great deal of experience in working with dyslexic and autistic pupils. Emily worked with the University of Brighton as a Professional Tutor and mentor to trainee teachers. Over the years, Emily has been a regular examiner for AQA. Emily now works full time on writing material and adding to the Revision Rocks range.

Customer satisfaction guaranteed: We want you to be entirely happy with our products. If for any reason there is a problem, please contact us directly: jeff.thomas@revisionrocks.co.uk and we promise to solve the issue.